flood

NICOLE KOOYMAN

FriesenPress

One Printers Way
Altona, MB R0G 0B0
Canada

www.friesenpress.com

Copyright © 2023 by Nicole Kooyman
First Edition — 2023

All rights reserved.

No part of this publication may be reproduced in any form, or by any means, electronic or mechanical, including photocopying, recording, or any information browsing, storage, or retrieval system, without permission in writing from FriesenPress.

ISBN
978-1-03-916442-0 (Hardcover)
978-1-03-916441-3 (Paperback)
978-1-03-916443-7 (eBook)

1. BIOGRAPHY & AUTOBIOGRAPHY, PERSONAL MEMOIRS

Distributed to the trade by The Ingram Book Company

To B.B.J.
&
Nellie,
who always told me when I was a little girl
that I should be a writer …

I wish you were here to see this.

Introduction

Natural disasters …

We hear about them. We see them on the news – long after the anguished stories of chaos and destruction have spread like wildfire on social media – categorized as "once in a lifetime" events.

It feels as if Mother Nature has taken notice of the online world. She appears more powerful and prevalent than ever.

We believe it will never happen to us: earthquake, fire, flood, sinkhole, tsunami (to name a few).

We rarely ask what happened before, during and after pleasant lives were upheaved. "How did you react? How do you cope? How do you recover when your 'it will always be there' comforts are taken away?"

The physical events of a disaster can be repaired. We can replant, rebuild, regrow and help heal new scars on nature's landscapes. The physical elements are the easy part.

But when rebuilding yourself, you're at the mercy of your own mind. When the mental wounds of a natural disaster cut deep, how do we heal our scars?

A true story …

- **Friday, October 29, 2021**
  7:50 a.m.

  "Have a nice day at school, kids! Have fun on Halloween at your dad's this weekend!" My truck pulls up to the curb in front of their middle school on a sunny, crisp October morning. All three, 15, 14 and 12, climb out chiming "Bye-eeeeee!" and catch up with their friends. I won't see them till next Friday.

- **Thursday, November 4**
  3:27 p.m.

  "Dad tested positive for Covid on Monday," my 15-year-old son says as he sits across from me eating his pre-work snack. His dad couldn't drive him, so I picked him up after school. I stare at my son and the very short distance between us, quickly recalling the hug we shared and the conversations we had in the truck. He looks up at me, mid-chew on his hamburger. "What?" he asks.

- **Friday, November 12**
  10:36 a.m.

  "Okay, Hun, I am ready to go," my husband says as he loads the last of his hunting gear into his truck. He wraps his arm around me and I melt into his tall frame. "I'll let you know when I get to Kamloops. Don't be afraid to call me if you have any problems in the barns." We kiss goodbye. I stand in the yard with my three dogs and watch him drive away. I'll be farming all 80,000 chickens on my own for the next five days.

- **5:06 P.M.**

  > *Environment Canada has issued a special weather statement: Heavy rain is expected this weekend in the Lower Mainland including the Fraser Valley. A series of moisture-laden systems associated with an atmospheric river from the Pacific will begin arriving Saturday evening and bring heavy rain to the south coast. Environment Canada is predicting anywhere from 75 to 150 mm of rain through to Monday morning.*

  "Atmospheric river?" What the heck is that? I've never heard that term before. It rains a lot all the time – it's fall – it's November ... we live on the "wet" coast – it rains 10 months out of the year here ...

  My Covid test came back negative. I still think my oldest son has a false positive. I talked to him on the phone and he said he has a headache. Is that from Covid? Or is he just stressed from being stuck at his dad's house all day and night? All three of my kids have to be in isolation at their dad's until the 20th of November. They will be retested on the 17th. That means they're also not in school. I'm worried about them, their mental health ... school is important for socializing too ... not being able to see their friends, hang out after school, go biking, to band, to the corner store ... it's going to be hard on them, and I really wish I could be there to help see them through it. At least I can talk to them on the phone, I guess.

  I've been up since 3:30 a.m. Having trouble sleeping again. Everyone is gone and I'm all alone. My husband left for hunting this morning. It's raining and I'm pretty bored and a little bit lonely. This weekend will be challenging for me; I struggle with depression and anxiety. Normally I can handle a few days on my own. Sometimes it's the most incredible thing, having the farm all to myself, doing what I want ... no one to interrupt me ... I guess I'm just off because of the kids and their being isolated. I feel helpless. I just want them home, but I can't get sick and my husband can't get sick. We don't know how this Covid virus could affect us if we got it – and neither one of us can be "down," not on a fully functional, operating farm with animals. There's no one to do our job for us if something happens. That's a lot of pressure. No, it's better this way. It doesn't feel like it, but I need to be reasonable. And being reasonable with a depressed, anxious brain is exhausting.

- **SATURDAY, NOVEMBER 13**

    What a day. I'm worn out and I didn't even do much. Chores, walked, played with the dogs, had a fire. These mental burdens are just as draining as physical ones. I'm trying so hard not to think about the kids. So I focused on the fire and the dogs, gave them lots of attention, talked to them, gave them lots of pets and cuddles. It started to rain just after lunchtime. I came inside and tried watching TV. I fell asleep and took a nap. Today was just an off day for me. I'm lightheaded, dizzy. Feeling fuzzy. Can't seem to "get going."

- **SUNDAY, NOVEMBER 14**

    Train wreck of a day. Chores were difficult. The birds were not moving as I tried to walk through the barns. I swear, every time you go in there, it's like they forget who you are, and they just sit and stare at you like they've never seen you before in their lives, when in fact, I've been there every day of their lives, twice a day. It has rained so much since yesterday afternoon; there's a lot of water on the ground surrounding the house. The entire garage flooded. My gym that I built for myself, all my workout mats, yoga stuff, all floating. I hope the treadmill will be okay. We've gotten lots of rain before, but not like this … this is a lot all at once.

November 14: Our main driveway and yard. Our garage to the left. Barn 2 straight ahead with birds in it.

- **12:54 P.M.**

    BC Highway 1, Highway 3 (Crowsnest), Highway 7 and Highway 5 (Coquihalla) are all closed due to mudslides and flooding from the rainstorm.

- **10:13 P.M.**

I'm texting my husband in panic mode. He took the Coquihalla when he left town for hunting.

His message reads:

How can I come home? Everything is closed and the worst is still to come tonight. I'll head towards Merritt in the morning and see what happens.

Okay. Maybe it's not that bad on the Coquihalla. Maybe they'll have it cleared up by tomorrow.

There have been mudslides along Highway 1 before that they've cleared up by the next day. I hope he can get through from Merritt. I wish he would just go now.

November 14: Our tractor barns (left) and my vegetable garden (right), completely submerged in water.

- **Monday, November 15**
  3:39 a.m.

  Text sent to my husband:

  Morning, Sweetheart. Well the winds came and that's what woke me up so early again. I just went outside to move the truck over by the shop away from the trees. It's scary out there. Like I'm trying hard not to be scared cause I know that's not going to change anything … I just want you to come home. Somehow. I don't care if you fly. Just come home.

  Received:

  Have to wait to see the next update on Hwy 1.

Sent:

I know. I'm sorry it's so early. Imagine being me right now that's all. I'm all the way down here, mother nature is losing her shit and I'm all alone. It's terrifying. The trees, the wind, the water.

- **10:37 A.M.**

    The entire City of Merritt is forced to evacuate due to flooding.

- **1:23 P.M.**

Text sent to my husband:

You need to start coming home now. Go through Pemberton (Highway 99). The Coquihalla is completely closed. There's a stretch of 4 lanes of highway that are completely gone.

They're gone! Princeton is under 6 feet of water!

Received:

Are you sure Pemberton is okay to travel?

- **1:27 P.M.**

    Mudslide Highway 99 Pemberton. All highways to the coast are shut down.

- **5:09 P.M.**

    Tank Hill – Highway 1 easst of Lytton – has washed away into the Thompson River.

This cannot be happening. This is some kind of sick joke.

Text received:

Working on a flight to get home.

Highway 1 (Trans Canada) closes in the Fraser Valley. Abbotsford Sumas Way east to No. 3 Road (our exit to get home).

He can't get a flight to Vancouver or Abbotsford. There's no way to get to our farm from either one of those airports because of the flooding in Sumas Prairie (where the highway runs). He has to get a flight to Chilliwack … How on earth is that going to happen? Chilliwack is just a little airport, not a major one like Abbotsford (YXX) or Vancouver (YVR).

This has been the worst weather storm I have ever seen. In the last 12 hours we have gotten more than 230 mm of rain. Now today we have 90 km/hr wind. All the highways out of the valley are closed. It's so scary right now being on my own. I've been reading online non-stop about what's been going on. Even worse, cellular networks have been going down so I can't even talk or text right now. I can't do anything. I'm stuck.

I'm stuck here and the kids are stuck in town at their dad's. I'm separated from them by a massive, flooded-out highway that's filled up all of Sumas Prairie. All those farms! The dairy farms out there! The cows! How are they getting out? Where are they going? I have no idea how bad it really is, but I do know that the water has gone OVER the highway – so that is deep! I know, I know, it's not good.

Okay. At least the kids are at their dad's, on top of the hill, with no potential for flooding. They're safe, in a house, with food, everything they need. It's okay, girl. It's okay.

Your farm is okay. You're not flooded.

- **Tuesday, November 16**
  2:54 a.m.

    Evacuation alert issued for our area of Sumas Prairie.

Excuse me – what? Evacuation alert? What does that mean? Is the water that much that it's coming our way? Do they know something that we haven't been told? I feel like there's a little tiny creature in my head running around in circles screaming, getting nowhere. What is going on out there?

- **10:56 A.M.**

    It's eerie on the farm. The everyday noises you get used to no longer exist right now. There's no highway noise. No road traffic. No tractors driving. Not a car, truck, feed truck, motorcycle, not even a pedal bike. It is quiet. My ears actually ring from the incredible silence, a silence you only hear when you're deep in the woods and you stop moving for a moment.

    I hear and see helicopters flying overhead, increasing as the hours pass. If the sound of helicopters flying above makes me feel nervous, when I know they're trying to figure out what's going on, I could never imagine living in a part of the world where the sound of a helicopter is a real threat.

    My husband managed to find a chartered flight to get home, a plane that would take him to Chilliwack. He actually connected with a friend of his up there, who was in Kamloops with his kids for a hockey tournament. Small world. So they're on their way home now. I'm so relieved he's making his way back. I'll feel a lot better having someone else here with me.

    I sit on the ground behind one of the barns and wait. It stopped raining a day ago. The skies finally parted and the sun came out for a bit – a welcome relief. Hopefully it'll suck up those massive puddles in our yard and driveway.

    One of my dogs, a bluetick coonhound named Duke, crawls onto my lap and decides it's a good place to take a nap. He's only five months old, he's still somewhat small enough and I let him. Welcome to being a farm dog, Duke … this rain won't happen every year, I promise.

Duke sleeping on my lap. Dozer, our three-year-old German shepherd, waits patiently.

- **12:30 P.M.**

After sitting with the dogs for about an hour, I get up and walk back between the barns and see my husband standing there at the feed bins. I squeak in surprise and run over. I hug him so hard I just don't want to let go. What a relief. He's home! He made it back!

He smiles and looks down at me. "We got a lot of work to do, Hun. C'mon, let's go."

Because of all the flooding, all farms in Sumas Prairie are being rationed with feed. We have our rations sorted out with the feed companies and are okay for now. As the highway west of us is shut down, we have to get all our feed from a company in Chilliwack, which is fine as they are currently feeding some of our barns right now.

We are not under water, but we've heard the dyke broke at McDonald Park (which is across the highway from where we are) and the ditches are filling. An evacuation order has been issued. We are being told we have to leave.

I went in the house and moved all valuables to higher ground while my husband worked on moving our freezers onto blocks and moving items out of the garage into our storage barn, which is a bit higher up than the garage.

The house is barren on the main floor and a complete disaster upstairs. I've been running as fast as I can to move everything I can lift up to the top floor.

I packed our travel trailer with essentials in case it becomes our temporary home away from home. We have yet to discuss when "the time" to go will be as we have been so busy moving our personal belongings to safer locations.

I've left the kids' stuff upstairs. I don't know when I'll see them. Everything that's important for them is safe. That's what matters.

As for our chickens, if we leave, there's nothing we can do for them.

To be clear – if we leave our evacuation ordered area – if we cross Boundary Road, we will not be allowed back to our farm.

Essentially, our local government just wants us to leave, and leave all our animals behind with whatever feed they have left.

The City of Abbotsford has shut the water off to our portion of Sumas Prairie because of multiple burst pipes. The water is contaminated with floodwater. At this moment, we still have water in our lines feeding our chicken barns.

So, not only does the city want us to leave our animals, they want us to leave them with no water.

I have been hearing (from social media) mixed reports of the Barrowtown Pump Station not working, that it's failing to keep up with the large volume of water. I am unable to confirm.

My husband and I are staying put for the moment, despite the evacuation order.

"We're not giving up on this farm or these birds," he says.

- **WEDNESDAY, NOVEMBER 17**
  5:29 A.M.

We are still at the farm, checking the ditches hourly, and they're holding.

Last night, Chilliwack Search and Rescue was at the Barrowtown Pump Station. We have friends who work for BC Hydro and Metric Civil Contractors. They were there all night, fortifying the station with sandbags, super sacks and lock blocks. They confirmed the pump station's status. Stupid social media. Why do people have to talk about things they know nothing about? I feel much better knowing what I know from people who are actually there right now.

Our city water has been shut off since 10:30 p.m. last night. We have plenty of bottled water and rain barrels, but our chickens have had no water.

No one is allowed in our area. They've set up roadblocks to stop people from coming into the prairie, as it's under evacuation order. The police are there, and when you leave, you're done; they won't let you back.

- **10:05 A.M.**

    Friends arrived with large water totes and pumps. I don't know how they got through, but they did. My husband attached them to the main water lines to the chicken barns. Chickens are getting some water for now.

    Large water totes with pumps. We will hook the pump up to the main water line that brings water to our chickens in the barns.

- **1:00 P.M.**

Abbotsford Police Department – URGENT PLEA: Within the last hour the water level within the eastern part of the Sumas Prairie is beginning to rise. Roadways that were dry an hour ago, now have flowing water …

- **4:47 P.M.**

    My husband has worked tirelessly all day along with friends to bring water to our farm for the chickens. What they've been doing so far has been working. We've been filling up our water totes from the dairy farm next door as they are on a different water system apart from the city water. We've also been siphoning out of our saltwater pool and mixing it with the tote water.

    I contacted the city regarding the water, and it turns out there are several broken water mains in Sumas Prairie. They are trying to address the broken water mains; however, any repair is likely not to happen anytime soon as the mains are under muddy, flooded water.

    The city will not allow feed trucks to come to the flats due to engineering issues of our roads, roads washed away and the integrity of bridges over our ditches. I'm not sure what that means for us. The only way in and out is via Keith Wilson Bridge off Boundary Road in Chilliwack, which is high and dry and has not been affected at all by the rains or floods. Feed could technically still come from Chilliwack. We are working on that.

    The floodwater from the west side of Sumas Prairie has rescinded, but it's pushing its way east towards us. Ditches have been slowly rising. We will monitor them through the night again. Barrowtown Pump Station is holding, but the Fraser River has not dropped enough to open the floodgates.

    The Nooksack River in the United States is still overflowing, which is causing our canals to flood and push the water to the east where we are.

    At this moment, we are both staying, although we have discussed the possibility of me leaving to be safe. I don't want to leave, knowing that, if I do, I may not be allowed back. And I'm not leaving my husband. I'm not being separated from him again.

    We're both tired.

    I'm exhausted.

We've only had six hours sleep total in the last three days. Been spending our nights running to the farm next door to fill water totes for our chickens, trying to keep them alive.

On top of all this – my kids had their Covid retest today. Even if they're clear, they still can't come home – there's no way to get here. They'll have to stay at their dad's a little longer. Hopefully they can go back to school.

At the dairy farm next to ours, filling a water tote. We bring this back to our farm, hook it up to the water lines, load an empty tote to the trailer and head back to refill it. By the time we fill and get back to our place, the tote previously hooked up is ready to be refilled again. It's an ongoing circle of back and forth. We are just able to keep up.

- **Thursday, November 18**
  7:21 a.m.

We moved our travel trailer to my in-laws in Yarrow. They are allowing farmers/residents to come and go to the evacuated areas so long as you provide proof of residence. Water has come up the ditches and is pooling on our lawns, heading towards the house.

We are still hand watering barns.

Apparently the Barrowtown Pump Station has opened its gates, which is good – but I haven't confirmed.

Water overflowing the ditches in front of our house and pooling in the yard.

- **8:16 A.M.**

Barrowtown Pump Station gates have NOT been opened. This is so incredibly stressful, hearing and reading rumours online. From now on, I'm only going to look at the City of Abbotsford's website and the Abbotsford Police Department.

The city is working on repairing broken dykes but can only do so if it's safe. And one of those broken dykes is across the highway from us.

I called the city and was advised that one water main has been located and they are working on a repair. It could take days. And that's only one of many that need repair.

No travel is allowed on Sumas Prairie for heavy trucks (that would be any fuel, feed or live haul). Today's rain is not important. Next week's weather storm will be the one to watch, an estimated 80 to 100 mm coming.

Water from the ditches flowing up our yard towards the house.

flood 18

- **7:28 P.M.**

    We spent the day getting water for our chickens.

    I talked to the emergency operations coordinator for our region, and he filled me in on a lot of information not shared on the news.

    We built a berm around our generator room. We also received a phone call from a local sawdust company that said they are able to provide "sock sacks," which are elongated sandbags filled with dirt. We are able to get them placed around our barn entries at ground level and the generator room. Our main focus today was protecting our generator room as it holds all sources of power to the farm.

    Our running back and forth to the dairy farm next door is no longer happening as we received a delivery of additional water totes from a company in Chilliwack.

    We received 10 water totes holding 1,000 gallons of water each. We also received water from the Greendale Fire Hall tanker truck to fill these totes.

Greendale Fire Department with their water tanker filling
our water totes hooked up to our chicken barns.

Unfortunately the groundwater has been slowly rising. It has filled the lawns and reached the base of the house. The water is coming up through our dirt crawl space. It has another full foot to go before reaching our living area.

Tonight, we will take turns sleeping, waking up to check on the water levels and pumping water from one tote to the other hooked up to our barn water system.

My husband and I have been doing this for three nights now.

Other farmers stopped by our farm. We gathered in the shop for a moment out of the rain. I had the woodstove going for some warmth. People coming by were people I had never met before. We all have a common bond – saving our animals and our farms.

flood   20

Some of these farmers are really young men, third- and fourth-generation farmers. I listened to them talk about how they did everything they could to get as many animals out as possible. Nothing breaks your heart into a million pieces more than watching a 20-something-year-old tear up when he talks about saving his cows. Every voice crack of emotional despair just broke me inside.

I found out later that one of them had to shoot several cows to put them down, as the animals could not be saved from the physical damage they endured from the flooding.

"Some of us are doing the Lord's work – while others are forced to drink the Devil's water."

My 14- and 12-year-olds' Covid tests came back negative. My 15-year-old's came back inconclusive. He will have to go again. I haven't seen my kids for 20 days.

November 19, 4:41 a.m.: Another all-nighter. Walking the yard with Dozer. Despite the disaster at hand, for a brief moment, the moon gives an eerie glow to something that feels like only a dream; however, it's very much a heavy reality.

- **Friday, November 19**
  8:36 a.m.

  During the night, the water came up from the east side of our property and headed towards the house. Yes, we have water in our crawl space, and it is slowly rising as it has been for the last few days, increasingly so during daylight. We had friends go around to all our barn entries with a sump pump to get the water pooling out and on the other side of the sandbags. There's no break from it, no sleep at night.

  Our focus is keeping the generator room and electrical for the property dry. We are in the process of obtaining more sandbags for the generator room. It is inevitable that some of our barns will be taking on water at some point today. It will be a slow rise.

  We are desperately trying to obtain the upper hand. Yes, there is talk of the city building levies; it won't be an instant fix. As slowly as the water came in – it will take just as long to leave. Even if the Fraser River drops and the Barrowtown Pump Station gates open, it will take days to get rid of what has accumulated on the prairie, and our end will be the last to see it go.

- **6:44 p.m.**

  The water filled our yard and all our driveways today. I walked around the yard and water came up to my knees, or higher, in some spots.

  So many people showed up today, familiar faces and total strangers with truckloads of sandbags. We were able to reinforce our barn doors and keep the water at bay.

  Water levels are holding. It has been all afternoon.

  We've been on city water all day, which means no more pumping from water totes.

  The kindness of strangers has been overwhelming. I have a pair of borrowed waders from a total stranger. We have an ample supply of sandbags. So far, minimal water has entered our barns. Our chickens are happy, healthy and completely oblivious to what's going on outside.

Last I checked, our house is still dry. We have a dry spot in the shop, meaning it's the only structure on this farm without water in it. The woodstove is still going.

While it's only 6:30 p.m. as I write, it feels like midnight. The days are becoming a blur.

Water starting to fill the driveway in front of the shop where we have a woodstove going to keep us as warm and dry as possible.

Water rising around the back side of our property, surrounding our barns with chickens inside. The black sandbags are what we put down initially. They won't be enough.

25   Nicole Kooyman

View from the main road in front of the house.
The main road, which is higher than our property, is dry.

The house and our front yard, with Dozer wading through the slowly rising water.

The back of our house, with pool shed (left) and our fish pond (middle).
The bricks on the highest portion of the pond are stacked three high.
The water has fully covered the first row.

flood 28

Our orchard (left), storage barn (centre) and vegetable garden (right).

View of the shop and tractor barn.

flood 30

Duke taking a nap in the last bit of dry he could find by the barn.

Signage from our security gate that came undone.

- **SATURDAY, NOVEMBER 20**
  10:25 A.M.

Thanks to volunteers, I was able to get a full night's sleep last night. I slept in my daughter's bed, in the house upstairs, for six hours. Even my husband got some sleep. This would not be possible without the help of friends to keep the sump pumps running around the farm all night.

Water levels have not changed, which is good.

This morning we heard that the Barrowtown Pump Station gates were opened at 2:00 a.m. We were able to confirm this information with onsite workers. We have also confirmed that a live haul truck is coming on Sunday night to pick up our chickens from the bottom floors.

Our next challenge is how to get the birds out of the barns. We have sandbags protecting our entries, and a forklift, along with chicken catchers, needs to get over these entries as there's two feet of water everywhere.

Volunteers at our farm placing sandbags higher around our bottom entries.

A barn empty of animals, as we were upgrading equipment. Had there been animals in this barn, they would have all died. Sandbags and sump pumps saved our bottom floors and the animals inside.

We spent the day putting more sandbags down.

We brought sawdust and wood pellets into the barns where water was seeping. We built a temporary wall to push the chickens out of the water towards the dryer floor. My husband and I will be staying up all night. We have no city water again, so we have to continue pumping water from totes into our barns. Our water filters are saturated with mud and debris. We have no access to our supplier for filter replacements, so we hand clean them as best we can for the time being.

My kids' Covid quarantine ends. My oldest has retested negative.

I am unable to pick them up as Highway 1 into town is still shut down. I decided it was better for the kids to stay at their dad's so they could at least go to school again on Monday, ending their nearly three-week isolation period.

A feed truck arriving. We were only able to get feed from the east of us (Chilliwack) as the highway was shut down.

- **Sunday, November 21**

    Some people from Yarrow came by to help manage our sump pumps around our barn entries, making sure they are running and shovelling water out of the way. The Greendale Fire Department refilled our water tanks.

    Our birds will start being shipped out at 1:30 a.m. We had to move some sandbags out of the way and build a ramp over the sand sock for the forklift to drive into the barn.

    It was another all-nighter managing the water totes.

    I fell asleep in the shop sitting in a chair by the woodstove. I slept from 5:30 a.m. to 8:30 a.m.

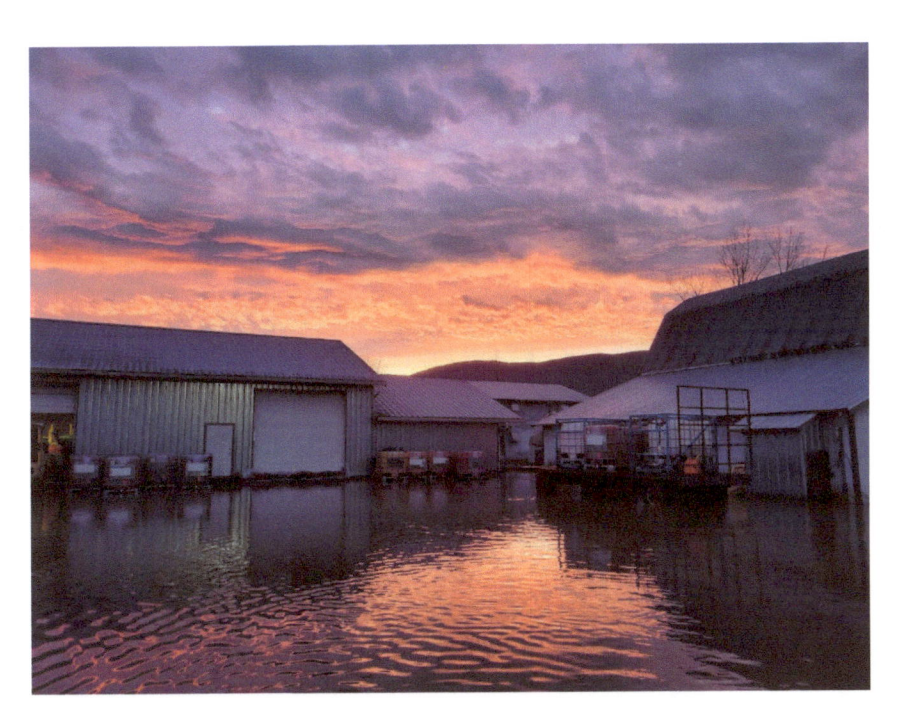

November 22: Walking out of the house to an inviting moment.

Sunrise over the shop and barn where our birds rest unassuming.

A brief pause to take it all in, trying hard to find some beauty among the disaster.

The last live haul truck leaving the yard. We had to empty five barns, just the bottom floors are gone. Those on our top floors will be picked up on Thursday night.

- **MONDAY, NOVEMBER 22**
  10:00 A.M.

It took over 24 hours since the floodgates opened for the water on our property to start going down. What a relief it was to be able to walk to the barns and not be up to my shins in water.

I cleaned out the dog pen today as the water has receded enough for us to start some minor clean-up. I swept all the water out, shovelled out their dog bed, put new bedding down of sawdust and hay, found all their toys, moved their feed buckets, set up the heat lamp. They're pretty excited to be back in their pen again rather than sleeping on the shop floor.

I moved into the house when it started to rain again and started putting things back where they belonged. I made our bed, put our furniture away. I am determined to sleep in my own bed tonight.

- **1:30 P.M.**

Received a phone call from my 15-year-old-son's school. He has been suspended indefinitely for a physical alteration on school property. They would not tell me any details at the moment. Today was his first day back to school after being gone for three weeks.

- **5:30 P.M.**

I just got off the phone with my 15-year-old. He sounded so distant and faded, exhausted and just beaten. You could hear it in his voice, the sounds of despair. He tells me he's worried he won't make it through the night. He's so distraught over being in isolation and what happened at school, he's talking about doing things to himself to "end" his pain …

I get him to promise me one thing – that if he finds himself in such a desperate state of mind, he goes to the hospital. No one will judge him, and he will be safe there, with people who will help him.

After we hang up, I call his stepmom right away.

I still have no way of getting to my kids. Highway 1 is still shut down and the only other way is through Agassiz (Highway 7), which also suffered damage during the heavy rains. Mudslides closed lanes, single alternating lanes in some areas; people are spending six hours in their cars to get through what should be, at most, a 45-minute drive.

I feel so helpless and sick to my stomach. I thought the worst was starting to be over with the waters rescinding. I can deal with the mess, the mud, the silt, putting everything back where it belongs; I can deal with the clean-up. I can deal with anything at this point ... anything except this.

- **10:00 P.M.**

My oldest son was brought to Abbotsford Regional Hospital and admitted to the psychiatric ward under the *Mental Health Act* after an attempt of self-harm.

Six months later

It's been a wet spring and so far the summer is proving the same. The damage to our property was minimal. The barns are okay, up and operational without skipping a beat.

Our furnace had to be replaced; my pantry is still torn apart. These little things I can deal with, when I know, for a fact, that some people still are not back in their homes.

During the holidays, as I unwrapped popsicle ornaments the kids made in their elementary school days, I thought of every person who suffered from the flood, and fires, who still were not in their homes.

I'm doing well not being on my medication. It was a rough couple months coming out of it. There were moments where I caught myself in old behaviours and thought patterns. I recognized them. I was able to tell myself, "It's just for now, not forever." I am able to overcome the intrusive thoughts. "They're just words," I tell myself. "That doesn't mean that they're true."

I do become slightly aggravated when I hear the term "atmospheric river" being tossed around like a beach ball. Social media and regular media do not help this situation. In one online group, I explained how these words could trigger anxiety and distress for those who actually went through the flood. They changed their post from "atmospheric river" and called it what it was – a heavy rainfall.

Across the highway from us, where the dyke broke and was repaired, there is water seeping into the fields. This makes me worry that it'll give way again. When a wall holding a river back breaks, it's pretty difficult to put that wall back up again; it's like threading a hose when the tap is wide open. I try not to think about this coming fall and the rain we always get. I know better than to sit in "what if" scenarios. I know we did it once; it can be done again.

After my son's admittance to Abbotsford Regional Hospital, they thought it best to send him to Surrey Memorial, to the Child and Adolescent Psychiatric Stabilization Unit (CAPSU). He remained there for a week, no visitors allowed.

The day of his discharge came a month after the last time I physically saw him.

I had to drive from our home, through Agassiz, to get to Surrey.

Walking into the CAPSU unit, I couldn't help but fight back the tears. All I could think about was my son's first day of kindergarten, how excited he was to go to school, saying goodbye as he waved enthusiastically with joy. I wished for the toddler days, where he asked me to watch *Cars* again or begged me for light-up shoes because they'd make him run faster.

How did we get here? How did any of these kids get here?

My heart shattered with every beat.

I am happy to say that, since his discharge on November 29, 2021, my son has been home, recovering well.

He proved he could do his schoolwork online and, in January 2022, was physically allowed back to school. He completed his grade, with honours, joined the school sports team and started a new part-time job.

As I sit and reflect on the last six months, it occurs to me that a flood is much more than just a physical act of nature.

Emotions and thoughts are just the same as a physical flood.

We have floods of thoughts, sometimes good, sometimes bad, and more often than not, the bad thoughts, like a broken dyke, become overwhelming and seem unstoppable.

But they do stop. They can be patched. There may be some seepage, but it's not total chaos, destruction and disrepair.

If we let it, we find a way. We move forward. Life carries on.

Afterword

It is really amazing, the things you can accomplish when you have no other choice.

I never thought I could stay up for four days straight, living off coffee, muffins and handfuls of trail mix in my pocket, wearing the same clothes for two days straight and spending 12 hours running around in water-filled boots.

When you are driven by an impending disaster, you don't have time. You don't have time to sit scrolling on your phone. Every second literally counts. The things you manage to persevere through – things you would never have thought you could ever accomplish on a normal day.

I used to take medication for depression. "Used to" being the key words. During this flood, I completely forgot to take my daily medication. It wasn't until a week had passed, when I started feeling strange (prescription detox), that I unwittingly realized what I had done.

Knowing the danger of starting again, I decided to ride it out. You'd think in such a moment of despair, distress and uncertainty, you'd need anything you could get your hands on to keep you calm, level-headed and feeling secure. Especially when living with a disease you can't physically see.

But I made it through.

We made it through.

My husband is the most resilient person I know. I've always admired him for how ingenious he can be sometimes, but during this disaster we went through, I saw a drive in him I've never seen from any human in my life. It was an indescribable determination and strength I don't think I could ever eloquently put into words.

There were more uncertain moments than certain ones. There was frustration and anger. There were apologies and tears. Through every moment, he still made the conscious decision to make sure I was okay, that I was eating, that I was getting enough sleep, regardless of what was going on, though his own basic needs were not being met.

We all have had moments where we feel like it couldn't get any worse – and then it does. We think that we can never pull through or recover. But it's our thoughts that determine our outcome. How we react is what helps us recover from adversity and major life changes. Resiliency is within all of us.

Acknowledgments

My husband and I would like to acknowledge the following people and companies who provided invaluable support and information during the flood.

Evan, Jordan, Angelica, Jim, Jeese, Mike, Paul and Pat.

Cedarwal Farms (Dave)
Pacific Dairy Centre – Chilliwack
Greendale Fire Department
City of Abbotsford – Operations Department
Abbotsford Police Department
Trouw Nutrition (John)
Ritchie-Smith Feeds (Mark)
Sunrise Farms (Kyle)
Metric Civil Contractors (Marlin, Chris)
BC Hydro (Jim)

Ted and Ria, for everything and anything we needed, supplies, food and sandbag help.

Thank you to the volunteers who stopped by, delivering sandbags, food and water. And thank you to those who stayed behind, total strangers, who helped keep the water out of our barns by managing sump pumps 24 hours a day.

I would like to thank the Abbotsford Regional Hospital Psychiatry Unit, Child and Adolescent Psychiatric Stabilization Unit (CAPSU) – Surrey Memorial, Emotions BC, Foundry, and BC Child and Youth Mental Health for all your support and your continued, dedicated work. My life depended on the kindness of several people; your work helped save more than one life.

Author Q&A with Michelle Superle, Associate Professor, Department of English Research Associate, Food and Agriculture Institute University of the Fraser Valley

MICHELLE:
Tell me a bit about your family and how you got into farming.

NICOLE:
My husband Mike has lived on the farm since he was very little. At the time it belonged to his grandparents, and then changed hands to his parents. Currently he runs all the farm operations as his parents retired in 2018 and moved to Yarrow.

I moved in with Mike in July 2013, we were married in October 2016.

Personally I grew up in the city of Abbotsford. Both my grandparents had farms, a nursery in Bradner and a blueberry/hobby farm in Matsqui. My only experience with farms was summertime visits. I certainly had no experience with animal farming.

Since I moved in, Mike has been working to teach me how to run an animal agricultural operation. There's no manual to follow. It's hands-on experience and time. To this day there is always something new that comes up that I have never seen or dealt with before. He's a good teacher and we work well together.

Michelle:
Tell me about your experience of the flooding.

Nicole:
Mike left for a 5 day hunting trip out of the valley, right before all the rain happened. I dropped my kids off at school Friday morning, they were going to their dad's for the week. I was on my own. I had farmed on my own before, for much longer periods of time. I was actually looking forward to a bit of quiet time!

My initial thought when the rain started was "This is a lot all at once" and "I hope if the power goes out the generator will run smoothly like it always does."

I was thinking of the mess I'd have to clean up after hearing the wind all night, knowing it was causing damage to the trees in the yard.

Next morning is when the flooding started in Sumas prairie.

When Hwy 1 shut down to Abbotsford I knew things were not good.

As the other highways to the coast started shutting down, that's when I knew I could be in trouble. Mike was in Kamloops, stuck there, all highways to the coast were closed. Fortunately he was able to get a flight to Chilliwack from Kamloops.

One thing I remember most after all the highways shut down, and after the weekend rain storm, there was one sunny day.

The sky was bright blue with a few clouds, it felt warm. I was sitting on the ground with my back against the barn tin. I could clearly see the Keith Wilson Bridge, which is normally bustling with daily traffic. I sat and watched the bridge. Not a single vehicle drove over that bridge. The silence made my ears ring.

There was no road traffic.

No tractors, no cars.

No highway noise.

Nothing.

It felt like I was in the middle of nowhere.

Then the helicopters came. First one, which is normal. Then another one, then another. Soon the sky was filled with at least a half dozen helicopters flying back and forth along Hwy 1.

When I saw that, my thought was "They're trying to figure it out" and "Something's not right"

It's really difficult to summarize everything that happened. Mike did make it home that sunny day, and the rest is written in the journal.

MICHELLE:
What makes you the most proud of how you've dealt with and are handling the situation?

NICOLE:
There was nothing about the situation that made me feel proud about myself. I was more thankful over the help that we received from family, friends and strangers from the community. I was thankful over how hard everyone worked to try to save us.

I feel pride when I create something, or set out to accomplish something and succeed. I suppose, now that it's over, I'm happy that I wrote everything down.

I'm proud of myself right now that I decided to reach out to a publisher to print my flood story.

MICHELLE:
What do you enjoy most about farming?

NICOLE:
I love having my space with no one else really being around. Walking out my back door is like walking in my own personal park every day.

Being farm managers gives us a lot of flexibility to try and squeeze in what we can. It's not always possible, because farm does come first, but for kids events and family functions, for the most part we can make it all work.

The downside is you could have plans, but if the farm needs you, plans get canceled. It could be 3am or when you're about to leave for a night out. For example, my husband has left the movies before because of a barn alarm.

MICHELLE:
What does a typical day of farming look like?

NICOLE:
There's no such thing as a typical day of farming. You get lucky that things go smoothly for a couple days, maybe even a week, but there's always something that happens.

On a perfect day I get up around 4-430am, because I like to have my coffee in peace before I head to the barn! I head outside at 5am and usually am back in the house around 630-7am to make sure kids are up doing what they're supposed to be doing before school.

After school drop off and returning home, I head straight to the office and allot myself till 10am to do paperwork, answer emails, track feed delivery schedules, payments etc. Sometimes after school drop off I have to go run and pick up parts or drop off equipment that needs repair.

The weather entirely depends on what's next. If it's nice out, there's always something to do outside. You could have barn entries to clean and disinfect. Because you have acreage, it doesn't just take care of itself. If the weather is poor (typically November to February) I have the luxury of having more time for myself.

In the afternoon after you get kids from school, you walk through the barns again. The age of the birds depends on how long it takes. The bigger they are, the longer it takes. Sometimes we don't get in until 7pm.

MICHELLE:
What sort of challenges do you encounter in farming?

NICOLE:
Challenges I have encountered farming are primarily flock health, ensuring the chicks are healthy and they haven't contracted or developed any disease that causes them pain or suffering.

Barn temperature maintenance is vitally important in that there's no swinging variables in temperature. I've had to fix barn heaters that quit working. I've had computers reset themselves for no reason and had to reprogram them.

Making sure our birds have access to water and the pressure is just right, which reflects on the quality of litter. Too wet and they could develop lesions or bronchitis. We had to deal with leaking water lines, water pipe explosions and plugged lines.

Feed getting into the barns and feeding out into the pans is important. It's an automated system, but I've had to fix feed triggers that won't start and feed motors that won't run. I've also had systems run all night long when they shouldn't have. There are safety switches, but it's never fool-proof.

Dealing with feed companies, for the most part, is flawless but human error does occur. Sometimes the wrong type of feed is delivered, or the delivery doesn't come at all, or it's put in the wrong bin. You have to know what your feed looks like, when it's supposed to be there so you can ensure if a mistake happens, it's caught right away and corrected. I've had to set an alarm for myself to wake up every 2 hours during the night to make sure a feed delivery came when it was supposed to, because an error occurred during the daytime.

MICHELLE:

What helps you meet those challenges?

NICOLE:

Meeting these challenges are purely based on experience. I had a great teacher (my husband) who's always showing me "this is what happened and this is how we fix it"

It's hard to remember everything he's taught me, but in the moment, if I quiet my thoughts, the answers come to me.

Silence is truly golden.

MICHELLE:

What are 3 words that describe your family values?

NICOLE:

I have always taught my kids from a young age to "be happy, be helpful and be kind."

When you're helpful and kind, you will be happy.

And when you are happy you are living your best life. Everything will fall into place.

MICHELLE:

When did you decide to evacuate your farm?

NICOLE:

Although we were under evacuation order, we never left our farm. We had animals in the barn, and relying on our barns to automatically do what they should do was not an option, given the challenges we face on a regular basis.

We wanted to try protecting our barns. At the time when we were told to leave, we had no sandbags and no way of trying to stop the water from damaging our structures.

That's when we found out the water supply was shut off. We couldn't let the feed automatically feed out, so many things could go wrong without monitoring, and if bins got empty, the system does not automatically shut off.

There was no way we were going to leave everything as is for who knows how long.

Michelle:

What are 3 words to describe what you were thinking and/or feeling as you were leaving your farm?

Nicole:

Cut off. Abandoned. Isolated.

During the flood there were road blockades set up to prevent anyone from entering the flood zone. Although we weren't in water yet, they refused to let anyone in to help us try to save our barns.

After mounting pressure from farmers, they allowed people in to help, only days after the evacuation orders were issued - so we lost that time where we could have done that much more to save our structures.

Michelle:

Before the November 2021 flood, had you ever wondered about what would happen if the Sumas Prairie flooded again?

Nicole:

Yes and no.

I thought more about how people try to redirect nature to suit our own needs.

You remove trees from a hillside for a building, there will be a landfall. Build a home by a river that erodes over time, it will wash away. Drain water, it will come back. Live in tornado country, you're going to get a tornado.

I find it fascinating that when these things happen, people are taken by surprise, as if we walk around every day with a 100% guarantee that none of these things would ever occur.

MICHELLE:
What thoughts and/or feelings arose as you were leaving your farm?

NICOLE:
Although we never left the farm, my husband wanted me to leave and be somewhere safer. The road blockade allowed us to move our travel trailer (stuffed with our belongings). Mike wanted me to stay with his parents, but I couldn't do it. I just went through the trauma of trying to get him home from Kamloops, I wasn't about to sit on the other side of a road block and be separated from him again.

MICHELLE:
What was the greatest challenge you faced when you first returned to your farm?

NICOLE:
Since we didn't leave our farm, we were able to start cleaning up right away.

Pressure washing and disinfecting the barns to get rid of all the debris was top priority. Thankfully it was a lot easier at this point for people to come and go through the barricades to help.

The process of just washing everything is a daunting task. Majority of things we had in storage that were in water had to be thrown away.

MICHELLE:

What are the main challenges you're facing on the farm now?

NICOLE:

Physically, nothing. We were able to get everything dried out as our flood damage was not as severe as what others had experienced.

I would say communication from the city and province about what they're going to do right now before they move forward.

It's great they're trying to figure out a long-term plan to improve things and make things better (like the pump station upgrade).

However, we all know that's going to take decades before anything ever begins.

It would be nice to know what their short-term solutions are to get us through to the end result.

I will not be surprised if something like this happens again within the next 10 years.

MICHELLE:

What do you want people to understand about your experiences in the flood?

NICOLE:

This is the most important message I would want anyone to really know.

Out of everything I've said, I would want people to know that during the flood, life still was happening for us. Throw in Covid, and you reach the point where, as I told Mike, "Something has to give and go away already" (my reference to Covid restrictions. While trying to get food, the last thing I'm thinking about is wearing a mask and social distancing)

Being cut off by a flood is beyond your control. Being isolated because of Covid restrictions is an imposition. When you smash the two together, it unleashes a mental shit-storm, and it feels like no one has ever really sat down and thought of the ramifications.

I have a teenage son, who not only was cut off from me and my home, he was under isolation because of covid restrictions (he did not have Covid - a member of his other household did). He was not able to see me, or come home, he wasn't allowed to go to school, see his friends, or leave the house either. For over 2 weeks of homebound isolation, there was a build up of highly stressful situations. They collided in an epic proportion so violently that he tried to take his life.

While I'm walking through 2 feet of water, stuck because the highways are closed, I'm begging my son over the phone to admit himself into the hospital for help. Thankfully he listened.

Life never stopped.

Cancer patients need treatment. Kidney patients need dialysis. Prescriptions need refilling, medication needs to be taken. Your payments still come out of your bank account. Your vehicle still needs fuel. Your kids look to you for reassurance, support and guidance. Your animals need you to keep them safe.

There's no worse feeling in the world like you're "stuck" on one side and everything else you need to survive is on the other.

MICHELLE:
What kinds of support would help you overcome the current challenges on the farm?

NICOLE:
We don't have any challenges specifically, but I feel that the mental health side effects of the flood is a huge challenge.

Not everyone is built the same and our coping mechanisms are not universal. If it was easier to access mental health care (counseling) I think a lot of people would be able to pull themselves through past and future challenges.

I know I sure could have used someone to talk too - but the costs for counseling is unaffordable, especially when you have a full household.

A lot of farmers, like myself, don't have benefit plans and packages to help alleviate the costs. Farmers also don't work 9-5 jobs. Although the core of our work could be flexible, sometimes it's just not possible to always leave and drive into town for a session.

Because of these reasons, farmers may not treat their mental health as a priority.

If mental health services were more flexible and conveniently available, I feel it could be utilized to a greater potential.

Personally, in an effort to try and sort things out, as it was more than just the flood that I was dealing with, I took it upon myself to do some self research.

It took me a while to find the right type of books for me that would help, but I was persistent and kept reading. I met some people who encouraged expressive writing.

This works for me, for many reasons. Primarily, I've always been creative and loved to read and write. Secondly, I had stubbornness within me to really see this through. I needed to get my mind straight, so I could be helpful to my family. If I'm not well, if I'm not healthy, mentally and physically, I'm not helpful to those who rely on me. That was my push.

Others may not be as fortunate.

And that's not right, for them to be left alone to fend for themselves.

Just like it wasn't right for us to be left alone to fend for ourselves when the flood happened, and help was refused to cross a blockade.

MICHELLE:

Which life experiences and values have served you well during the crisis?

NICOLE:

There was no life experience that could have prepared anyone for something like this.

Actually, the best thing I did for myself was to not think. I didn't think of anything. My mind was blank like an empty blackboard.

Without thinking I had no worry. Not thinking kept me from ruminating about what had happened. It also prevented me from panicking over "what it" scenarios for a future that hasn't happened yet.

It was like a light switch. Instead of turning it on and filling my head with ideas - I shut it off and made it dark.

MICHELLE:

Who's part of your support system?

NICOLE:

My husband is always first and foremost my support system. He's always there for me, I can talk to him about anything no matter how big or small. He's intuitive enough to know when I might need something, and is always there to try and make things good. "I just want to see you happy," he always says. I wouldn't be where I am today if it weren't for him. I could write a whole other story of how he has literally saved my life.

I'm thankful for all the friends and family who were there for us, even for the little things. It's the little things that build your foundation for the big support. One of my friends who lives in Keremeos called me at 530am on her way to work and talked to me during the flood event. That was so helpful, just hearing about something else other than what I was currently going through.

I have to be my own support system as well. At the start of the flood, I was on my own. I realized I'm not always going to have someone there to help me all the time. If I want to keep moving forward in life, I'm going to have to learn how to support myself.

I started to read about the brain, brain functions, cognitive behavioral therapy and overall finding out more about how the brain works and its thought processes.

I am the type of person who likes to know how things work and reasons why. I couldn't think of a better way to provide support for myself than to study the one machine that runs me daily.

I began to write as well, which has been a tremendous help in articulating exactly what I'm thinking and feeling.

MICHELLE:
What have you learned about yourself throughout your experience of the flooding?

NICOLE:
In a moment when things don't go according to plan, it's easy to get upset.

I have learned that whatever is happening in the physical world, is happening. That's it. It's happened. And there's no amount of thinking that can undo what has or has not happened. So, what do you do?

I've learned to stay in the present moment. Thinking about the past will not undo the past. Worrying about the future won't change whatever is about to happen.

Staying in the moment, focusing on right here, right now, is all I can do.

Instead of looking hard for answers, I turn off that light switch of thoughts, and let them come to me.

I've learned to trust my initial thought and instinct more, instead of arguing, second guessing or rationalizing with myself.

I've learned to take a step back sometimes in order to discover the next step forward.

Most important, I fail at all of these things all the time. What I'm getting better at is recognizing when I've fallen off track. I'm able to pick myself up to that place of present peace where I want to be.

Life continues to flow.

I just chose not to fight the current.

Flooding on the Lower Mainland can be seen from space. (Chris Hadfield/Twitter)

Satellite image of the flooded Sumas Prairie. Our farm is circled in yellow. Far left is the Sumas Drainage Canal. The Barrowtown Pump Station is across the canal on the top left. This photo leaves me at a loss for words, how we came so close to deep water overtaking our property. Its difficult to keep the mind still and not be overrun with what-if scenarios. We were one of the lucky ones. I'll take it.

flood   62

CPSIA information can be obtained
at www.ICGtesting.com
Printed in the USA
BVHW010108070323
659790BV00001B/1